AF228851

XTREME ROBOTS

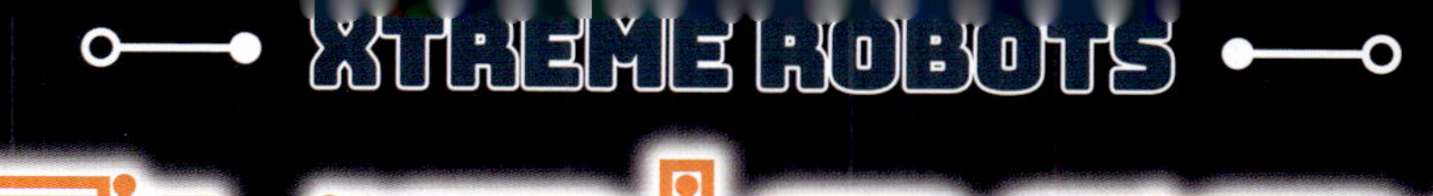

Explorer Robots

S.L. HAMILTON

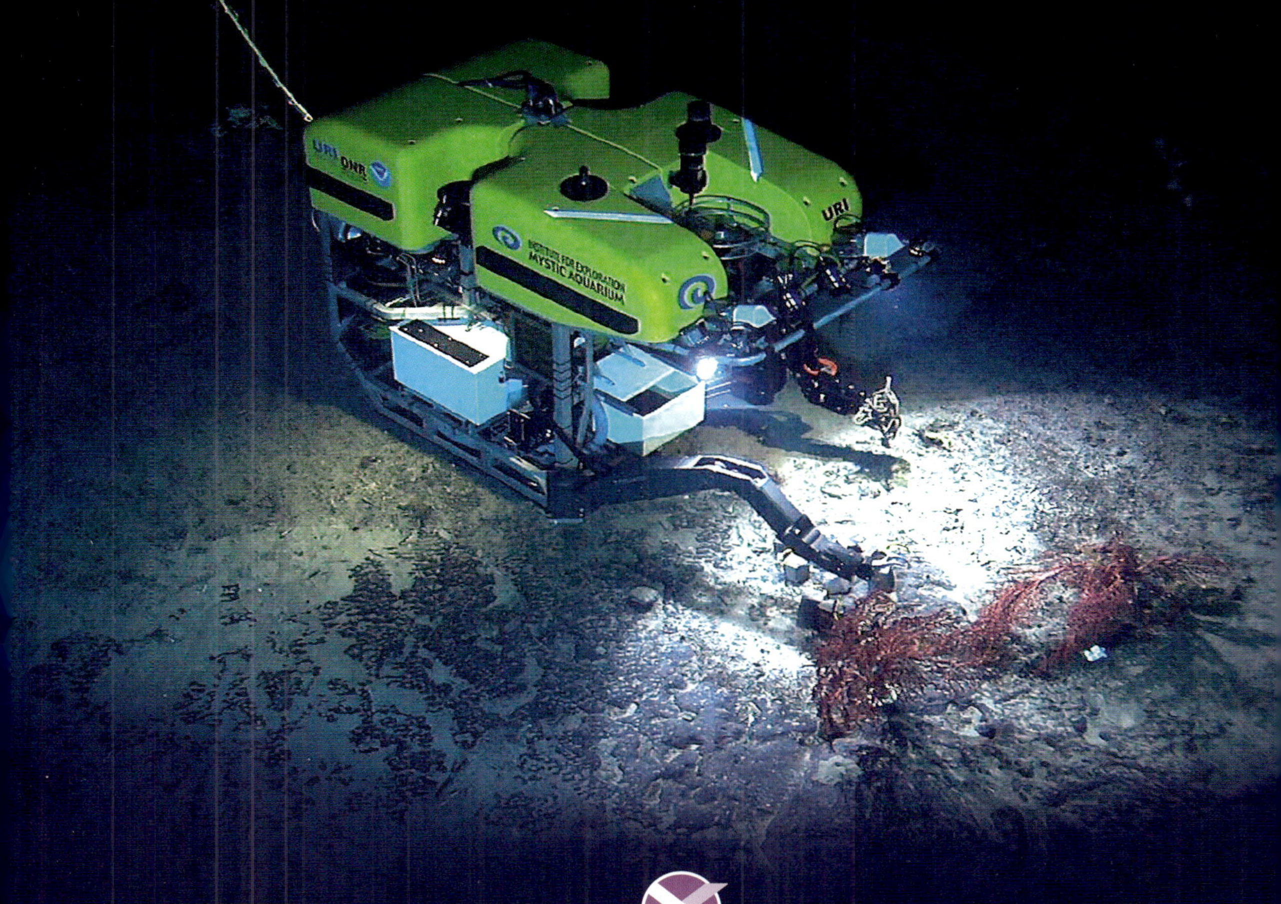

A&D Xtreme
An imprint of Abdo Publishing | abdobooks.com

abdobooks.com

Printed in the United States of America, North Mankato, MN.
102018
012019

Editor: John Hamilton
Copy Editor: Bridget O'Brien
Graphic Design: Sue Hamilton
Cover Design: Candice Keimig and Pakou Moua
Cover Photo: AP
Interior Photos & Illustrations: Carnegie Mellon University/Howie Choset/
Nico Zevallos/Chaohul Gong-pgs 18-19; Freiberg University of Mining and
Technology/Saxony Ministry for Science and Art/Mining RoX Project-pgs 16 & 17;
Inria-pgs 20 & 21; NASA-pgs 14, 15, 22, 23, 24, 25, 26, 27, 28, 29, 30 & 31;
NOAA-pgs 1, 8, 9, 12 & 13; OpenROV/David Lang/Eric Stackpole-pgs 2-3, 6 & 7;
Shutterstock-pgs 4-5; U.S. Navy-pg 32;
Woods Hole Oceanographic Institution-pgs 10 & 11.

Library of Congress Control Number: 2018950012
Publisher's Cataloging-in-Publication Data

Names: Hamilton, S.L., author.
Title: Explorer robots / by S.L. Hamilton.
Description: Minneapolis, Minnesota : Abdo Publishing, 2019 | Series: Xtreme
    robots | Includes online resources and index.
Identifiers: ISBN 9781532118234 (lib. bdg.) | ISBN 9781532171413 (ebook)
Subjects: LCSH: Robot vision systems--Juvenile literature. | Robots--Juvenile
    literature. | Robotics--Juvenile literature.
Classification: DDC 629.892--dc23

Contents

Explorer Robots

Robots can go where it is too dangerous or impossible for humans to explore. These mechanical adventurers are found deep under the sea and far out in space. They also work in mines, caves, under ice, and in hot volcanoes. They help people learn more about our world and the universe.

Undersea Robots

Many people want to explore what lies under the water. Robots called unmanned marine vehicles (UMVs) can dive into watery depths. Some are programmed to explore by themselves, or autonomously. Some UMVs have human operators.

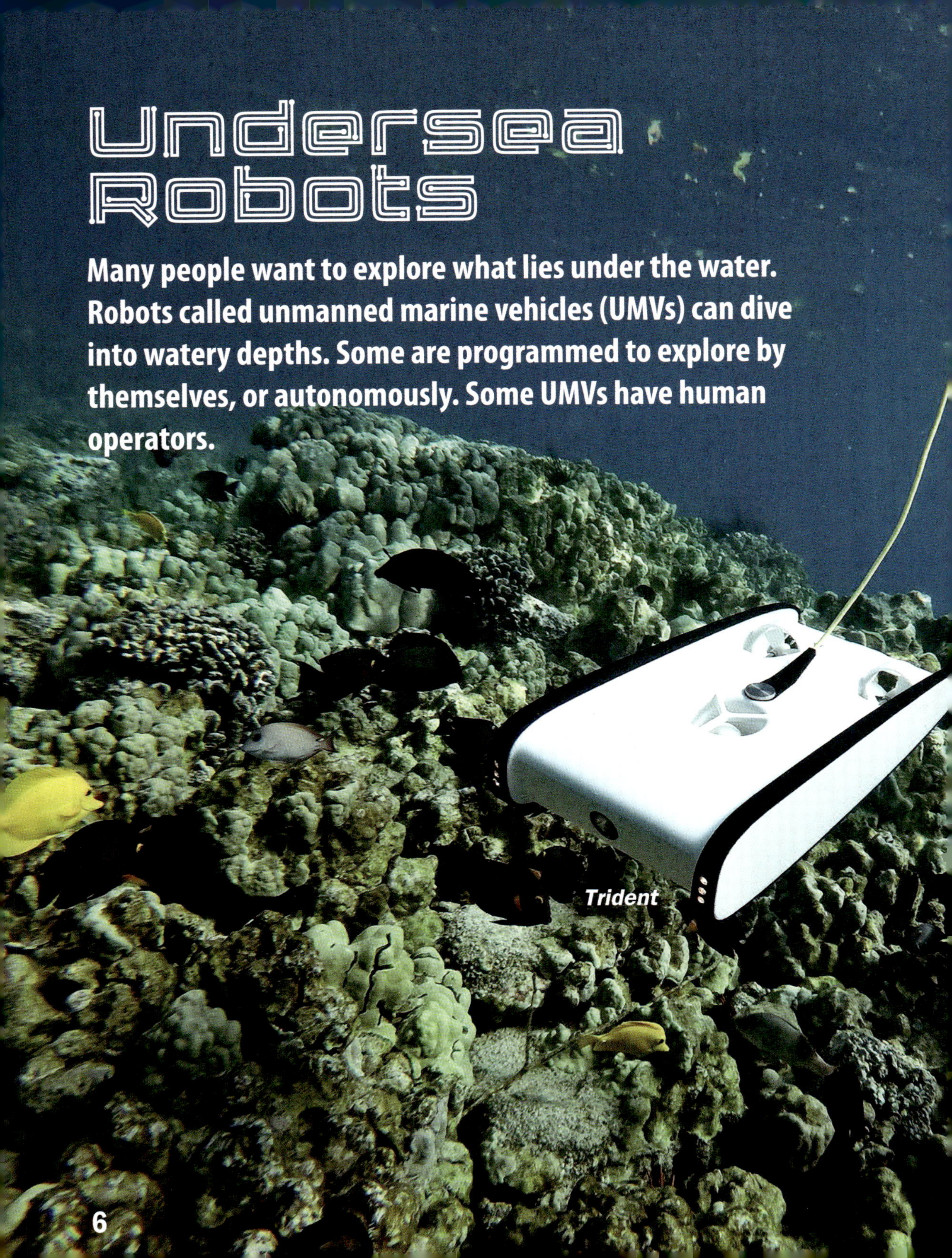

Trident

Trident is an underwater robot created by OpenROV. This explorer robot is operated by a single pilot. It can dive as deep as 328 feet (100 m). It is battery operated and can stay underwater for up to 3 hours. It can move fast, zooming along at 6.6 feet per second (2 meters per second). Or it can hover in place to get a good look around. It has a thin tether that sends video footage to curious explorers.

XTREME FACT – David Lang and Eric Stackpole wanted to explore an underwater cave. There was a legend that the cave might have hidden gold from a robbery in the 1800s. They built their own diving robot to do the exploration. They didn't find gold in the cave, but they started their own company, OpenROV (remotely operated vehicle).

Deep sea exploration robots can go where people would be at risk. Human divers are limited by the amount of air they have and water pressure on their bodies. Global Explorer ROV (remotely operated vehicle) can reach ocean depths of 10,000 feet (3,048 m). It has a tethered power cable and can stay down for hours.

XTREME FACT – SCUBA divers often limit themselves to a depth of 130 feet (40 m). The deepest a human diver has gone is 1,090 feet (332 m). Ahmed Gabr took 12 minutes to go down and 14 hours to come up. He had to stop every few feet to decompress. He carried 9 air tanks.

The Global Explorer ROV is equipped with lights, plus video, still, and 3-D cameras. It has a collection claw and a slurp gun designed to gently gather specimens and artifacts from the seafloor. The samples are placed in insulated drawers onboard the ROV to be taken topside for scientists and researchers to study.

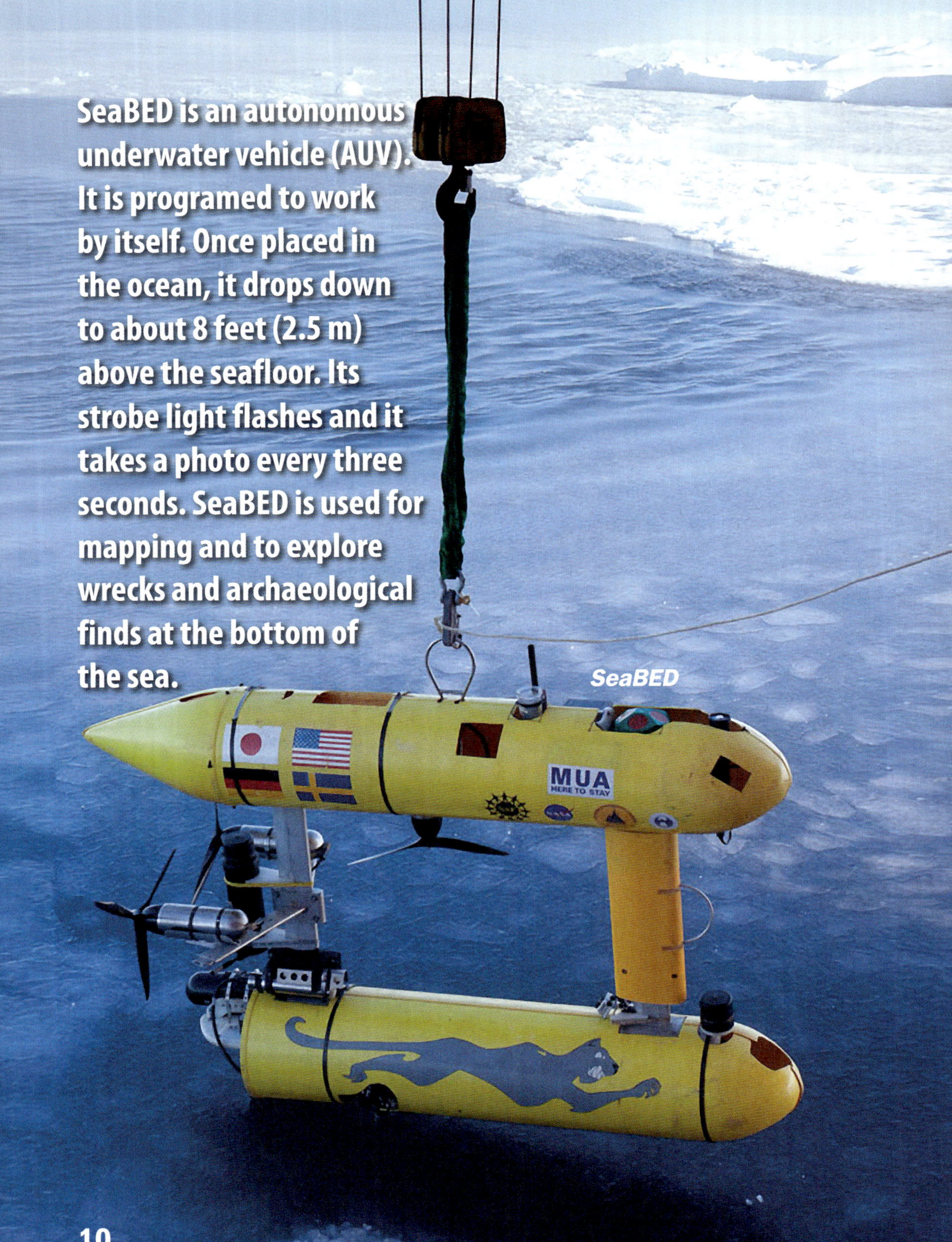

SeaBED is an autonomous underwater vehicle (AUV). It is programed to work by itself. Once placed in the ocean, it drops down to about 8 feet (2.5 m) above the seafloor. Its strobe light flashes and it takes a photo every three seconds. SeaBED is used for mapping and to explore wrecks and archaeological finds at the bottom of the sea.

XTREME FACT – SeaBED can go as deep as 6,562 feet (2,000 m). It moves at a steady speed of .6 miles per hour (1 kph). It has been put to work exploring shipwrecks and under the ice in Antarctica.

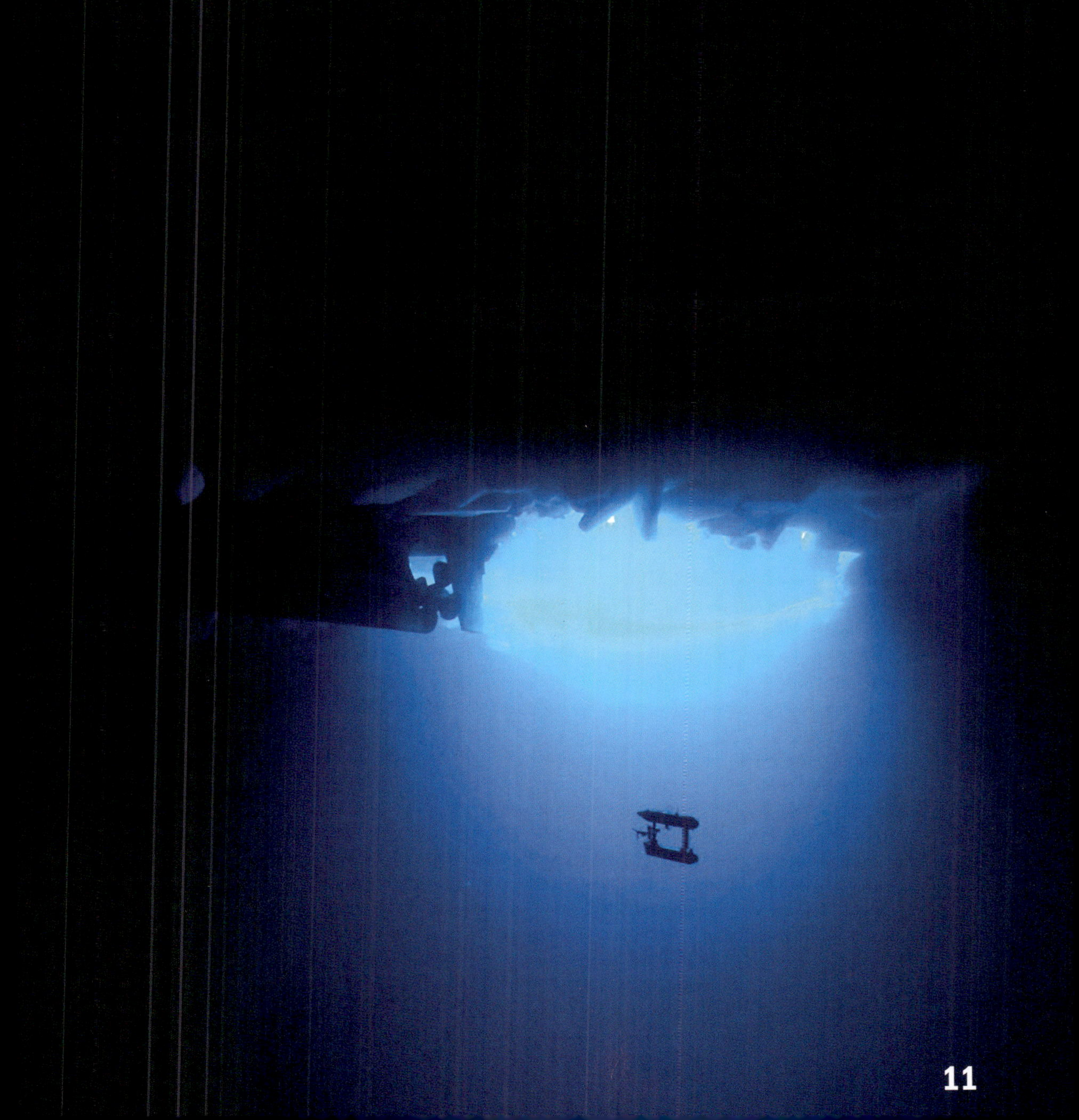

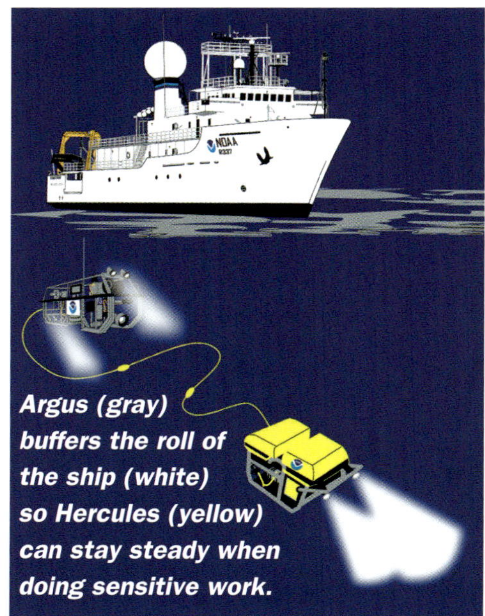

Tandem ROVs (remotely operated vehicles) are robots that work connected to each other.

The *Nautilus* Exploration Program uses tandem ROVs "to explore areas of the ocean that have never been explored before." Argus is a towsled-style ROV. It has lights and cameras. Its main job is to keep Hercules steady when the yellow ROV is doing sensitive work. Hercules can go as deep as 13,123 feet (4,000 m). The ROV's six thrusters move it in any direction a researcher wants the robot to go. The ROV has still and video cameras that can zoom, pan, and tilt. Its suction tube and two arms collect samples and artifacts on the ocean floor. The specimens can be stored in onboard boxes and brought to the surface.

XTREME FACT – About 95% of Earth's oceans are unexplored.

Volcano Robots

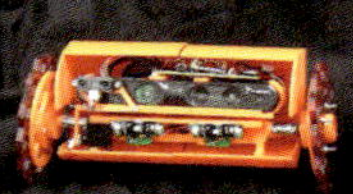

VolcanoBots 1 and 2 were developed at NASA to do the dangerous work of exploring inside volcanic fissures. A fissure is a crack where magma is most likely to erupt. In 2014, VolcanoBot 1 was sent down into Hawaii's Kilauea volcano. The 12-inch (30-cm) -wide, wheeled robot rolled down as deep as 82 feet (25 m) to create a 3-D map of the inside of the fissure. It did not make it to the bottom. The smaller 10-inch (25-cm) -wide VolcanoBot 2 has been designed to go deeper into a fissure. It has a live video feed to let operators move the robot. The information these robots gather may help scientists learn to predict future eruptions.

VolcanoBot 1 in a lava tube.

In 2014, NASA researcher Carolyn Parcheta sent VolcanoBot 1 into a then-inactive fissure in Hawaii's Kilauea volcano. Mapping the inside of a fissure will help scientists learn how magma comes out of the ground. This may help predict future eruptions.

Cave and Mine Robots

Robots help explore caves and mines. Humans are at risk when they venture deep underground. Dangerous and explosive gasses lurk unseen. Cave-ins are possible. Cracks in the ground can go down for hundreds of feet. Exploration robots can map mines and caves. They can take air-quality samples. Robots can check to see if a mine contains the natural resources that make it worthwhile to continue operations.

A look at Alexander's mapping ability.

Julius and Alexander are exploration robots developed by Germany's Freiberg University of Mining and Technology. Julius is equipped with a three-fingered gripper that operates devices designed for human hands. It assists miners in scanning for radiation and taking other readings. Alexander is an autonomous robot programmed to explore and map mines on its own. It is equipped with cameras, lights, and scanners. These mining robots can go where it would be dangerous for humans.

XTREME FACT – *Robots programmed to explore caves and mines are known as "subterranean robots."*

Archaeology Robots

A robot snake can get into dangerous areas and through small openings where humans cannot go. These explorer robots can be used by archaeologists. Carnegie Mellon University's serpentine robot, Elizabeth, was brought to Egypt to explore some man-made caves. It was thought the now sealed-off chambers stored ancient ships. Elizabeth slithered over rubble, rough surfaces, and through tight spaces. However, the robot snake could not move well over the sand. It did not get into the caves.

XTREME FACT – When engineers use a life-form in nature to create robots, it is called biomimicry.

Elizabeth, the robot snake

The mysteries of Egypt's Great Pyramid of Giza have inspired archaeologists to turn to robots for help. Possible voids, or open areas, may exist inside the massive limestone and granite tomb. Scientists do not know if they are really there. An explorer robot could be sent in with video and still cameras to see what's really inside the Great Pyramid and other ancient structures.

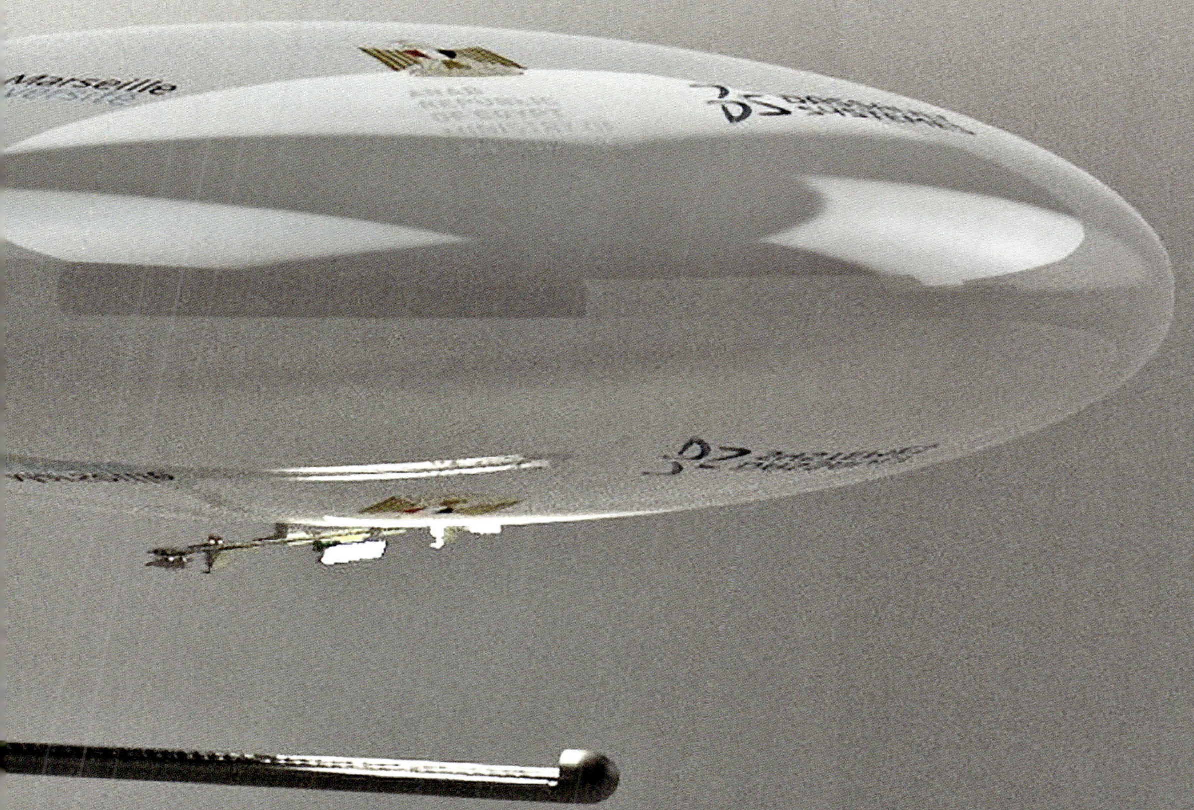

By drilling a small hole through the pyramid, a tiny robot can go in with lights and cameras. A helium-inflated "blimp" would carry it around to see what no one has seen since 2560 BC.

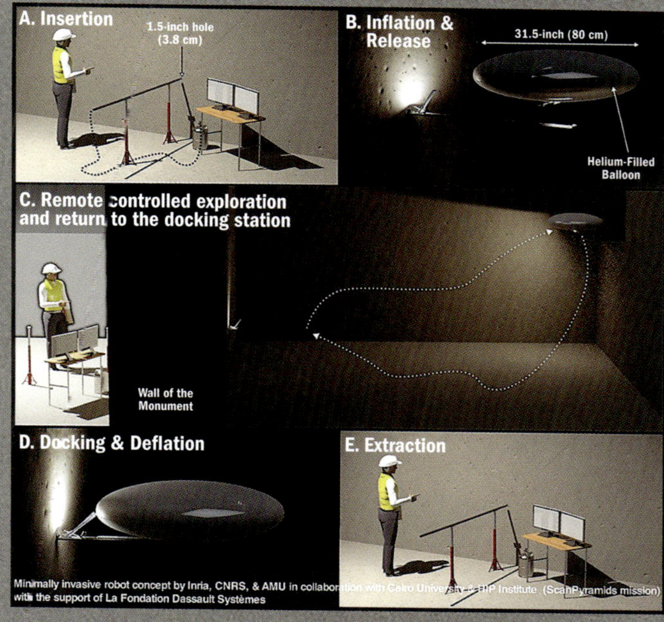

Space Robots

Space exploration is dangerous. Brave astronauts take great risks to explore the unknown. Many robots have been developed to help. Probes, orbiters, landers, and rovers go to cold, airless, radiation-exposed planets, satellites, and asteroids. Robots do some of the exploration work that might kill humans.

NASA built a prototype Lunar Truck. The robotic vehicle was made to move across the Moon's surface with an active suspension and six pairs of wheels. It is fitted with exploration equipment and can be driven by an astronaut.

Astronauts last walked on the Moon in 1972. NASA has a mission to get back to Earth's satellite. Engineers developed Resource Prospector (RP) to help achieve this goal. RP was built to drill in the Moon's poles, looking for hydrogen, oxygen, and water. These resources could help humans go to Mars. Although RP may not go as originally designed, its tools will likely be used for robotic surface missions.

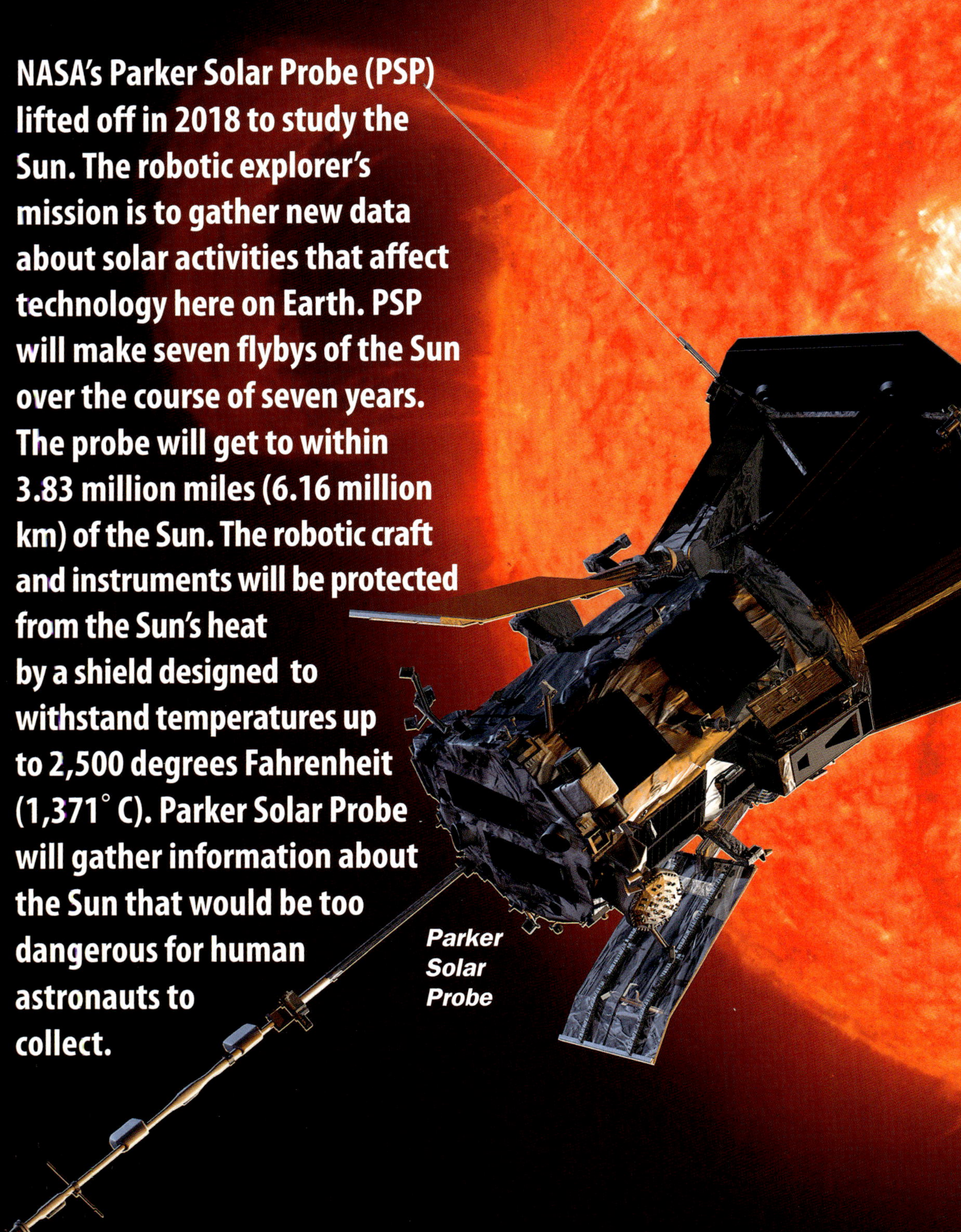

NASA's Parker Solar Probe (PSP) lifted off in 2018 to study the Sun. The robotic explorer's mission is to gather new data about solar activities that affect technology here on Earth. PSP will make seven flybys of the Sun over the course of seven years. The probe will get to within 3.83 million miles (6.16 million km) of the Sun. The robotic craft and instruments will be protected from the Sun's heat by a shield designed to withstand temperatures up to 2,500 degrees Fahrenheit (1,371° C). Parker Solar Probe will gather information about the Sun that would be too dangerous for human astronauts to collect.

XTREME FACT – At its closest approach, Parker Solar Probe will hurtle around the Sun at approximately 430,000 miles per hour (692,018 kph). That's fast enough to get from Philadelphia, Pennsylvania, to Washington, DC, in one second!

Curiosity rover reached the surface of Mars on August 6, 2012. It is the size of a small car, and the biggest rover ever sent to Mars. The robotic explorer's mission is to test the Martian soil, rocks, and air to see if Mars has the right conditions to support tiny life-forms.

XTREME FACT - Curiosity's descent from the top of the atmosphere to Mars's surface was called "seven minutes of terror." It took that long for NASA scientists to get word that Curiosity had landed safely.

Curiosity is a rolling science lab. It can analyze rock, soil, and air samples. It has a radiation detector. It is equipped with 17 cameras. Its 6.9-foot (2.1-m) -long robotic arm features a close-up camera, drill, rock-cleaning brush, and a scoop for gathering samples. Curiosity was built to last two years, but as of late 2018, it has been exploring Mars for more than three times its expected life. Its work will help future astronauts reach Mars.

NASA continues its work on exploration robots. An under-ice robot called BRUIE (Buoyant Rover for Under-Ice Exploration) is being tested in dangerous glacier areas on Earth. BRUIE can both float in the water and roll along the underside of ice with gripping wheels. The robot's cameras and lasers can scan and map never-before-seen areas. BRUIE can test for radiation. It may one day explore Europa, one of Jupiter's moons. Europa is covered by an icy crust. A liquid ocean lies beneath. BRUIE can drill down to see if there is life in the cold oceans of a distant world.

Hedgehog's sensors.

Hedgehog isn't a typical exploration robot. It is designed to hop and tumble around rough, uneven terrain without being damaged. Its instruments work no matter which way it lands. Hedgehog may one day explore an asteroid or comet. These rocky space objects do not have much gravity. Hedgehog's spikes allow it to turn in place. If it falls into a deep hole, it has a "tornado" spin that launches the robot out of trouble. Exploration robots will help pave the way for future human explorers.

Glossary

ARCHAEOLOGIST
A person who searches for, uncovers, and studies artifacts from the past in order to learn how people once lived.

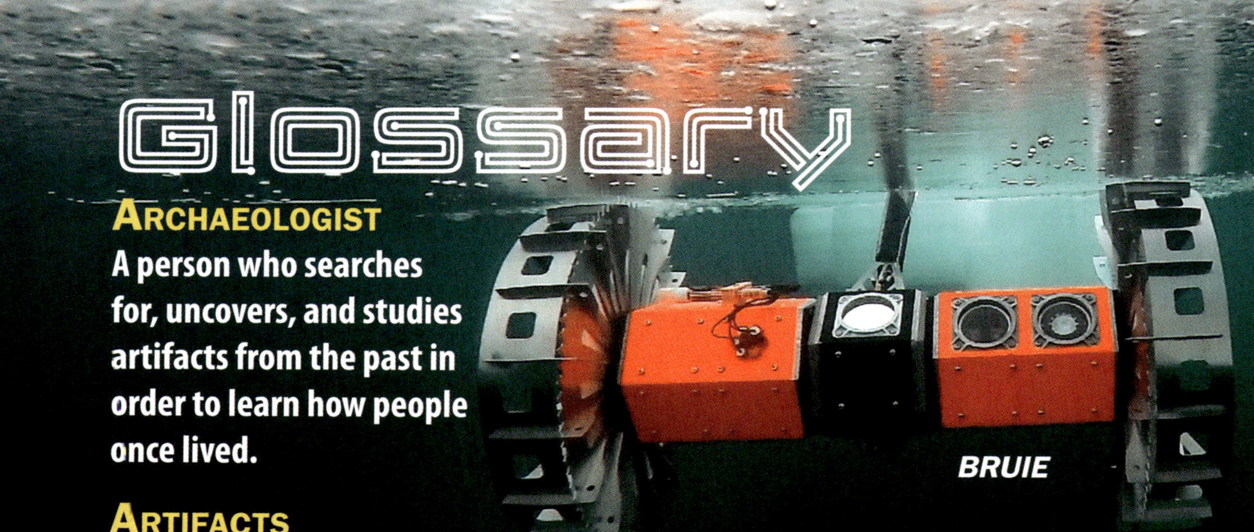

ARTIFACTS
Objects from the past, often items made by humans.

AUTONOMOUS
Able to work on its own. An autonomous robot does not have a human operating it. Its programming allows it to do its job without help.

BIOLUMINESCENT
Light given off by life-forms in nature, such as deep-sea fish.

DECOMPRESS
For deep-sea divers, to make stops every few feet as the diver rises back to the surface. This allows the reduction of gases that have built up inside the body. If this is not done, painful bubbles are created inside the body. This is called getting the "bends."

ENGINEER
A person whose job is to use scientific knowledge to create and maintain mechanical and electronic objects and structures. This includes such things as robots, cameras, and engines.

MIMIC
To do something the same way as something or someone else does it.

NASA (**N**ATIONAL **A**ERONAUTICS AND **S**PACE **A**DMINISTRATION)

A United States government space agency started in 1958. NASA's goals include space exploration, as well as increasing people's understanding of Earth, our solar system, and the universe.

RADIATION

A kind of energy that comes from a radioactive source such as uranium. It can cause sickness or be fatal to people who are exposed.

SCUBA (**S**ELF-**C**ONTAINED **U**NDERWATER **B**REATHING **A**PPARATUS)

Equipment that allows divers to breathe underwater.

SENSORS

In robots, devices that send out signals and get information from a surrounding area. The robot's computers may use the data to decide what the robot should do next, or pass the collected information on to a human operator.

TETHER

A connecting rope or wire. In robots, it may be used to keep an object from moving too far away or as a way to get power to the robot.

Online Resources

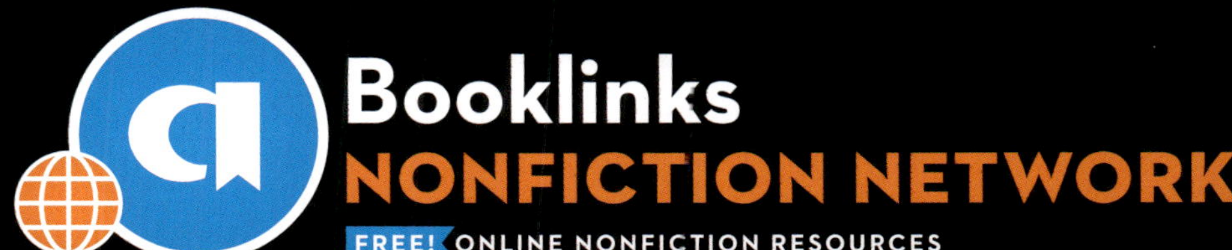

To learn more about explorer robots, visit abdobooklinks.com. These links are routinely monitored and updated to provide the most current information available.

Index